I Can Do Money Word Problems

Rebecca Wingard-Nelson

CONTENTS

Coins and Bills

 penny
1¢

 one-dollar bill
$1

 nickel
5¢

 five-dollar bill
$5

 dime
10¢

 ten-dollar bill
$10

 quarter
25¢

 twenty-dollar
bill
$20

Money Word Problems

You can solve word problems about money using four steps.

1. Read the problem.
   Jacob has 2 dimes and 3 pennies. How many cents does Jacob have?

2. Plan how to solve the problem.
   What does the problem ask you to find?
   How many cents Jacob has.

   How can you find the answer?
   You can count the value of the coins Jacob has.

3. Follow the plan.

Count the value of the coins. First count by tens for the dimes. Then count on by ones for the pennies.

| 10¢ | 20¢ | 21¢ | 22¢ | 23¢ |

Jacob has 23¢.

4. Check your work.

Did you use the right coins? *Yes.*
Count the value of the coins again.
Is your answer the same? *Yes.*

How Much in All?

Read the problem.

Ben had 50¢. He found a quarter.
How much money does Ben have in all?

Plan how to solve the problem.

What does the problem ask you to find?
How much money Ben has in all.

How can you find the answer?
*You can add the amount Ben
started with and the amount
he found.*

Follow the plan.

How much money did Ben start with? *50¢*
What did Ben find? *A quarter.*
What is the value of a quarter? *25¢*

Started with   50¢
Found   + 25¢
                      75¢

Ben has 75¢ in all.

Check your work.

Did you use the numbers from the problem?
Yes, Ben started with 50¢.

Did you use the correct value for a quarter?
Yes, a quarter is worth 25¢.

How Much Is Left?

Read the problem.

Sienna had $6. She used
$2 to pay for her lunch.
How many dollars does
Sienna have left?

Plan how to solve the problem.

What does the problem ask you to find?
How many dollars Sienna has left.

How can you find the answer?
*You can subtract the amount Sienna spent
from the amount she started with.*

Follow the plan.

Sienna started with $6.

She spent $2. Subtract $2.

$$\begin{array}{r} \$6 \\ -\ \$2 \\ \hline \$4 \end{array}$$

Sienna has $4 left.

Check your work.

Did you start with the right amount? *Yes, $6.*

Did you subtract the right amount? *Yes, $2.*

Check your subtraction using addition. 4 + 2 = 6, correct.

Who Has More?

Read the problem.

Trina had 3 dimes and 4 pennies. Annie had 1 quarter and 3 nickels. Who had more money?

Plan how to solve the problem.

What does the problem ask you to find?
Who had more money.

How can you find the answer?
Count how much money each girl had. Then compare to see who had more.

Follow the plan.

How much money did Trina have?
She had 3 dimes and 4 pennies.
Count the value of 3 dimes and
4 pennies. Trina had 34¢.

How much money did Annie have?
She had 1 quarter and 3 nickels.
Count the value of 1 quarter and
3 nickels. Annie had 40¢.

Which is more, 34¢ or 40¢?
40¢ is more than 34¢.
Annie had more money than Trina.

Check your work.

Count the value of each girl's coins again.
Did you count the same amounts? *Yes.*

Can I Buy That?

Read the problem.

Barack has 3 dimes and 14 pennies.
A marker costs 39¢. Does he have
enough money to buy a marker?

Plan how to solve the problem.

What does the problem ask you to find?
If Barack has enough money to buy a marker.

How can you find the answer?
*First find the value of 3 dimes and 14 pennies
by adding the value of the dimes and the pennies.*

*Compare this amount to the price of a marker
to find out if Barack has enough to buy the marker.*

Follow the plan.

How much is 3 dimes and 14 pennies worth?

$$3 \text{ dimes} = 30¢ \qquad\qquad 30¢$$
$$14 \text{ pennies} = 14¢ \qquad \underline{+\ 14¢}$$
$$44¢$$

Barack has 44¢.

A marker costs 39¢. Barack needs 39¢ or more to buy a marker. 44¢ is more than 39¢.

Barack has enough money to buy a marker.

Check your work.

Did you answer the right question? Yes.
Count the coins. Did you get the same answer? Yes.

Is This Enough?

Read the problem.

Emily has a ten-dollar bill. A poster costs $5. A book costs $6. Does she have enough to buy the poster and the book?

Plan how to solve the problem.

What does the problem ask you to find?

If Emily has enough for a poster and a book together.

How can you find the answer?

You can add the cost of the poster and the cost of the book to find what they cost together.

Then compare the cost and the amount Emily has to find out if she has enough.

Follow the plan.

Add the cost of the poster, $5, and the cost of the book, $6.

$5 + $6 = $11

The poster and book together cost $11.

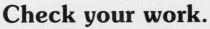

Emily has a ten-dollar bill.
A ten-dollar bill is worth $10.
Emily needs $11 or more to
buy the poster and book together.
$10 is less than $11.

**Emily does not have enough to
buy a poster and book together.**

Check your work.

Did you add correctly? Yes. *5 + 6 = 11*

How much Change?

Read the problem.

Bubble gum costs 35¢. Rachel paid for it with
2 quarters. How much change did Rachel get back?

Plan how to solve the problem.

What does the problem ask you to find?
How much change Rachel got.

How can you find the answer?
*Start with the amount Rachel used to
pay for the gum.
Subtract the price of the gum to find
the change.*

Follow the plan.

Rachel paid for the
gum with 2 quarters.
2 quarters = 50¢

25¢   50¢

Start with 50¢.

Subtract 35¢.

$$\begin{array}{r} 50¢ \\ -\ 35¢ \\ \hline 15¢ \end{array}$$

Rachel got 15¢ in change.

Check your work.

Check your subtraction by using addition.

Add the amount of change, 15¢, to the cost of the gum, 35¢.

$$\begin{array}{r} 15¢ \\ +\ 35¢ \\ \hline 50¢ \end{array}$$

The sum is 50¢. This is the same as the amount
Rachel paid. The answer is correct.

Change From a Dollar

Read the problem.

Ethan bought a seashell at a garage sale for 64¢.
He paid with a one-dollar bill. He was given the least
number of coins possible in change. What coins
did Ethan get as change?

Plan how to solve the problem.

What does the problem ask you to find?
The coins that Ethan got as his change.

How can you find the answer?
*Subtract to find the
amount of change.
Decide what coins were
used to make the change.*

Follow the plan.

Ethan paid with a one-dollar bill, worth $1, or 100¢.   100¢

He spent 64¢.   − 64¢

Ethan's change was 36¢.   36¢

Make 36¢ using as many of the most valuable coins as you can without going over.

One quarter is worth 25¢.

25¢

35¢

36¢

One dime more is 35¢.

One penny more is 36¢.

Ethan's change was 1 quarter, 1 dime, and 1 penny.

Check your work.

Count the value of the coins you used.

Do they equal 36¢? Yes.

Counting Change

Read the problem.

You sold a candy bar for 79¢. You were paid with a one-dollar bill. You gave back 21¢ in change. How can you count back the change to show that it is correct?

Plan how to solve the problem.

What does the problem ask?
How you can count back change.

How do you count back change?
Start with the amount something costs, then count on. When the change is all counted, the total should be the amount that was paid.

20

Follow the plan.

The cost of the candy bar was 79¢. The change was 21¢. Let's say you used 2 dimes and 1 penny to make the 21¢ in change. Begin with 79¢. Count on, starting with the lowest-value coins.

Begin with: 79¢
Now count on: **80¢**   **90¢**   **$1**
                                                            (or 100¢)

Since you end at $1, and $1 was the amount that was paid, the change is correct.

Check your work.

Did you use the right coins?
Yes, 2 dimes and 1 penny make 21¢.

LET'S REVIEW

Solve word problems using four steps.

    1. Read the problem.
    2. Plan how to solve the problem.
    3. Follow the plan.
    4. Check your work.

Add money amounts to find a total.

Subtract money amounts to find how much is left when some is spent, or how much change you should get.

Count back change, starting with the amount spent. The ending amount should be the same as the amount that was given to pay.

LEARN MORE

Books

Dalton, Julie. *Counting Money*. New York: Children's Press, 2006.

Ziefert, Harriet. *You Can't Buy a Dinosaur With a Dime: Problem Solving in Dollars and Cents*. Brooklyn, NY: Blue Apple Books, 2003.

Web Sites

The Change Game
    <http://www.apples4theteacher.com/change-game.html>

Money Math Games
    <http://www.gamequarium.com/moneymath.html>

INDEX

Enslow Elementary, an imprint of Enslow Publishers, Inc.

Enslow Elementary® is a registered trademark of Enslow Publishers, Inc.

Copyright © 2010 by Enslow Publishers, Inc.

All rights reserved.

No part of this book may be reproduced by any means without the written permission of the publisher.

Library of Congress Cataloging-in-Publication Data

Wingard-Nelson, Rebecca.

    I can do money word problems / Rebecca Wingard-Nelson.

        p. cm. – (I like money math!)

    Summary: "An introduction to money word problems for young readers"–Provided by publisher.

    Includes bibliographical references and index.

    ISBN 978-0-7660-3145-6

    1. Problem solving–Juvenile literature. 2. Word problems (Mathematics)–Juvenile literature 3. Money–United States–Juvenile literature. I. Title.

    QA63.W5576 2010

    513–dc22

                           2009006490

Printed in the United States of America

10 9 8 7 6 5 4 3 2 1

ISBN-13: 978-0-7660-3659-8 (paperback)

ISBN-10: 0-7660-3659-6 (paperback)

Photo Credits: Shutterstock

Cover Photo: Shutterstock

Enslow Elementary

an imprint of

Enslow Publishers, Inc.

40 Industrial Road

Box 398

Berkeley Heights, NJ 07922

USA

http://www.enslow.com